FUN
with
Electronics, Jr.

by
Luann Colombo
& Conn McQuinn

Illustrations by
Kaz Aizawa

Andrews and McMeel
A Universal Press Syndicate Company
Kansas City

From the *Fun with Electronics, Jr.*, packaged set, which includes electronic parts, wires, and this book. *Fun with Electronics, Jr.* is produced by becker&mayer!, LTD.

Book and package design by Suzanne Brooker

ISBN: 0-8362-0597-9

Other children's kits from Andrews and McMeel by becker&mayer!:
  The Amazing Sandcastle Builder's Kit
  Build Your Own Dinosaurs
  Fun with Ballet
  The Ant Book & See-Through Model
  The Bat Book & See-Through Model
  Build Your Own Bugs
  Amazing Airplanes Book & Kit
  The American Appaloosa
  The English Thoroughbred
  Fun with Electronics
  Sleeping Beauty

CONTENTS

Note to Parents (and older kids too)

The parts in this kit will allow you (and your children) to explore the basic concepts of electricity. While the experiments are written for very young children, they will be interesting to kids of all ages (and grown-ups too). For older experimenters, more detailed explanations in the *What's Going On* sections encourage a higher level of understanding. To better help your children learn from using this kit, here are a few simple rules:

1) Let the kids build the projects! We know it looks like fun, but this is supposed to help them learn! (You can experiment when they're in bed.) Help them with the directions if they get confused, help them troubleshoot if they get stuck, but let them do the work.

2) Ask them questions. Why does the light bulb light? What does the push button do? How did you wear out the batteries so fast?

3) Let them ask you questions—and don't be embarrassed if you don't know! The information within the book will help you answer many of the questions children will ask. Take a minute to read the *What's Going On* sections so you can show the kids that learning doesn't end when you leave school.

4

4) Encourage them to invent their own projects. Once they know how to use the kit and understand even two or three of the projects, suggest that they apply their knowledge. Use the light bulb in a little paper lighthouse. Use the motor in a cardboard helicopter. The more they experiment and create, the better they will understand.

Remember, the projects should be fun. A warm fuzzy feeling about science and experimenting would be the best results of all!

Warning!: Do not use any other source of electricity with your projects. Use only AA batteries. There is no risk from the current in your batteries, but anything more powerful will fry the parts of your kit— at the very least. Handle electricity with extreme care.

WHAT IS ELECTRICITY?

We use electricity every day. It makes our clocks run. It makes our lights glow. It makes our toast hot and our milk cold. It makes our TV work (which is very important!). Electricity is the power that runs hundreds of things.

But what is electricity?

Everything in the world is made from very, very tiny things called atoms; rocks, trees, books, birds, water, ice cream, cat food, and even you! Atoms are so small that nobody can see them.

Even though atoms are very, very tiny, they have parts that are even smaller. One of the parts is called an electron (ee-lek-tron). All atoms have electrons. And electrons are where electricity comes from.

Sometimes an electron can be pushed from one atom onto another atom.

When that electron moves from one atom to another, it makes a tiny little bit of electricity. To make the kind of electricity we can use, it takes many, many electrons jumping between many, many atoms.

We're Electricity!

WHAT'S IN THE TOOLBOX?

Let's see what's in your kit:

two 3-way connectors

six 2-way connectors

battery case

(holds 2 AA batteries—not included)

light

motor

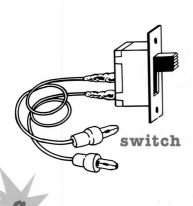

switch

push button

LED

spinning disk

buzzer

(makes a really annoying sound)

Eventually, you will use all of the parts. Put them in the box for now and take out each part as you need it. Keeping a clean work space will make life much easier. It's hard to find things in a plate of electronic spaghetti.

SAVE THE CARDBOARD BOX! It has punch-outs of a spiral, fan, and other stuff that you'll be using later.

The cardboard box workbench is also the motor stand to hold your motor!

9

HOW TO USE THE CONNECTORS

It is easier to make electrons move in metal than in plastic, rubber, glass, or wood. That is why electrical things use metal wires.

The wires in your kit have special ends to make it easy to plug them together. Take out the battery case and look at it. You will see that the wires coming out of it have little plugs with round ends. If you look back in the toolbox you will find six connectors which are small metal tubes with plastic covers.

They fit right on the ends of the plugs. You will use them to connect the wires to each other, just like in this picture. Make sure your plug fits tightly.

Because the connectors are metal, the electricity will go through them easily.

What's Going On?

Electricity flows through metals. They (whoever "they" are) say that metals can conduct electricity. These materials are called conductors. Plastic, rubber, and glass are poor conductors. They are electrical insulators and are often used to cover conductors such as metal wires, just like yours.

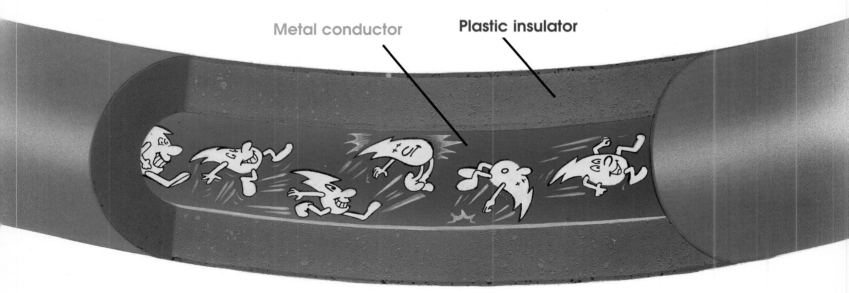

Metal conductor

Plastic insulator

Ready? Let's try the first project!

A BRIGHT IDEA

To build your first project, look for these parts:

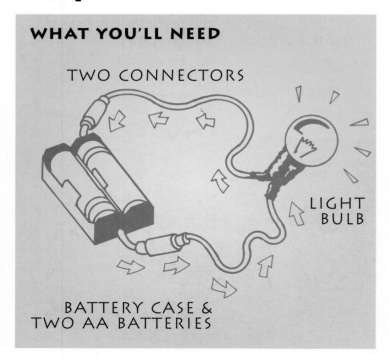

WHAT YOU'LL NEED

TWO CONNECTORS

LIGHT BULB

BATTERY CASE & TWO AA BATTERIES

Look in the battery case and you will see two little springs. Now, look at the batteries and you will see that one end has a bump. The other end is flat. Put the batteries in the case so the flat ends touch the springs.

Take the two small connectors and put them on the ends of the battery case wires. Now, plug the ends of the light bulb wires into the connectors.

It lights up!

Be careful! Don't leave the light on for very long because it will get warm. Also, it will wear out your batteries, and you won't be able to do any more projects! To turn it off, just unplug one of the wires.

What's Going On?

The electrons coming out of the black wire go into the red one. When you make the electricity go through the light bulb, it goes through a tiny little wire. Look closely at the bulb, and you will be able to see the wire inside. Pushing all those electrons through that wire makes it very hot. It gets so hot that it glows!

Unhooking one of the wires makes the light go off. Why? Because the electricity has to have a place to start and a place to go. If both ends of the battery case aren't connected to the bulb, it won't work.

When all of the wires are connected, it is called a complete circuit. That means the electricity can get from the black wire in the battery all the way to the red wire.

TIME TO SWITCH

When you turn off the light in your house, you don't have to unplug it. You use a switch.

There is a switch in your kit that looks like this!

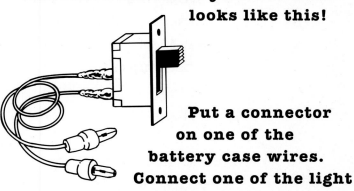

Put a connector on one of the battery case wires. Connect one of the light bulb wires. Put a connector on the other light bulb wire. Connect the switch. Put the last connector on the other switch wire. Connect it to the battery case.

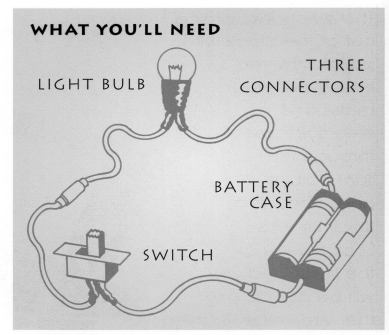

WHAT YOU'LL NEED

LIGHT BULB

THREE CONNECTORS

BATTERY CASE

SWITCH

If the light didn't come on when you connected the wires together, push the switch button over. Now the light should come on! You can turn it on and off, just like a lamp.

14

What's Going On?

Inside the switch is a little piece of metal. When the switch is ON, the little piece of metal touches both of the wires that go into the switch. This makes a bridge that lets the electricity go through.

When the switch is OFF, the metal doesn't touch the wires, and the electricity can't go through. So it stops!

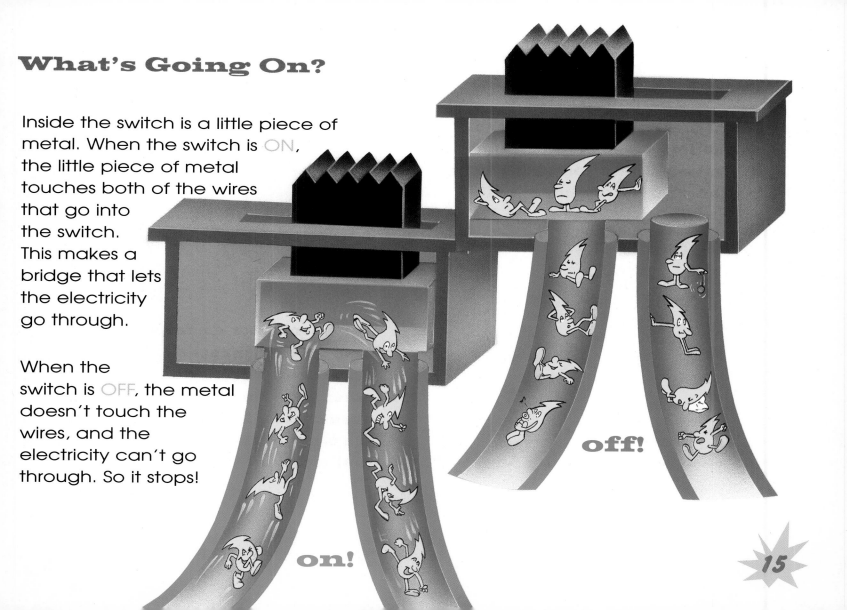

on!

off!

15

PUSH THIS BUTTON

Sometimes you want a light to come on for just a few seconds. A push button allows you to do this. Find the push button in your kit.

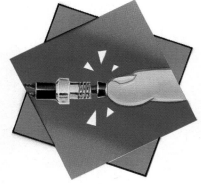

WITH A PUSH BUTTON YOUR LIGHT STAYS OFF UNTIL YOU PUSH THE BUTTON. FOR THIS PROJECT, YOU NEED A STRONG FINGER TO PUSH THE BUTTON.

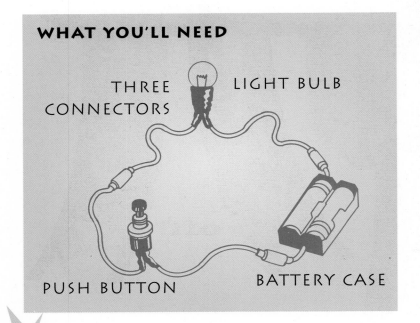

WHAT YOU'LL NEED

THREE CONNECTORS

LIGHT BULB

PUSH BUTTON

BATTERY CASE

Put a connector on one of the battery case wires. Connect one of the light bulb wires. Put a connector on the other light bulb wire. Connect the push button. Put the last connector on the other push button wire. Connect it to the battery case.

What's Going On?

There's a little piece of metal in the push button. When you press on the button, that metal touches both the wires in the push button. Just like in the switch, this makes a bridge that lets the electricity go through. When you let go of the button, the metal pulls away from the wires and the electricity can't go through. So your light goes out.

on!

off!

LET'S GET MOVING

Now that you have made a light bulb turn on and off, you're ready for some **ACTION**. Motors use electricity to make things move.

Fit the plastic disk onto the motor (make sure it's a snug fit; you wouldn't want that thing to go flying when you turn on the motor). Punch out the place for the motor on your workbench and set the motor in the hole. Put connectors on the battery case wires. Connect one of the motor wires. Put a connector on the other motor wire. Connect the motor to the push button and the push button to the battery case.

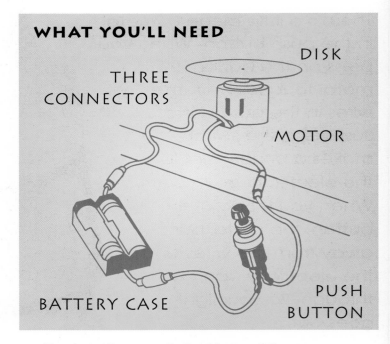

WHAT YOU'LL NEED

DISK

THREE CONNECTORS

MOTOR

BATTERY CASE

PUSH BUTTON

Press the push button. Oh, we forgot to tell you—the motor will spin. So be careful to keep your fingers out of the way.

What's Going On?

There are small magnets in a motor. When you put electricity in a motor you create more magnets inside the motor. These magnets are called electromagnets. They are attracted and repelled by the other magnets that are already in the motor, which makes them spin.

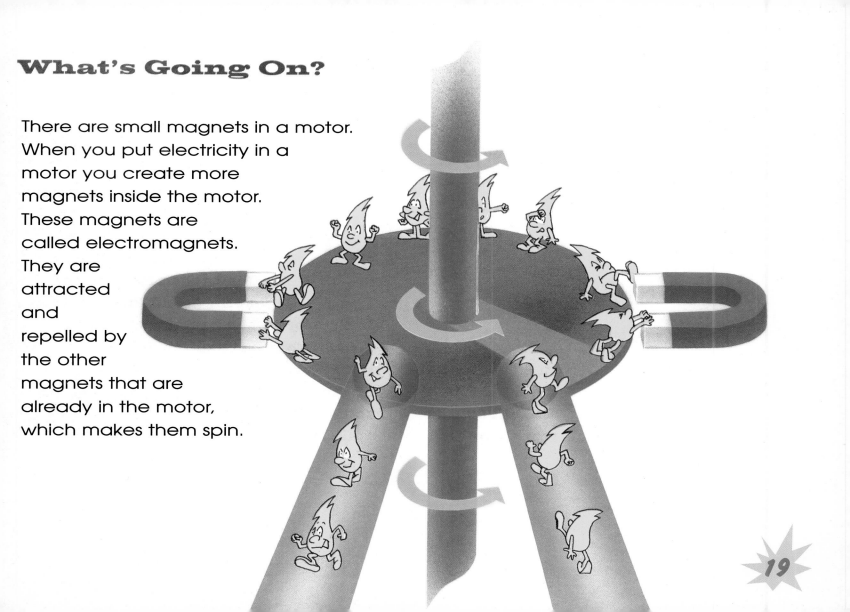

NOW FOR SOME WHEEL FUN

With a motor that spins a round disk, there are all kinds of colorful experiments you can do.

WHAT YOU'LL NEED

DISKS
CRAYONS
MARKING PENS
(TO MAKE MORE DISKS:
CARDBOARD, TAPE, & SCISSORS)

Punch out the round disks from the back of your cardboard workbench.

Take the disk that's half blue and half yellow. Press the paper disk firmly onto the motor so that the plastic bump goes into the hole on the disk. Place the motor in the motor stand and connect the motor to the batteries. Watch what happens to the colors. Do the blue and yellow combine to make green?

What's Going On?

The motor spins so fast that our brain reads the two colors together. Just like what happens with paint and the seal on Ziplock bags: Blue and yellow make green.

LET'S EXPERIMENT

What other colors will mix? Color the blank circle half red and half blue. Tape this one to the disk and connect the motor. Do the colors mix to make purple?

Attach the spiral disk. Watch it spin, and also watch the spiral as it slows down. Swap the wires to see if the spiral goes in the other direction.

Use a round disk as a pattern. Trace several circles on a piece of paper. Cut them out. Color a circle half black and half white. Tape it to the motor disk and see what happens. Look for a difference when you hold your spinning disks under a regular (incandescent) light bulb or under a fluorescent tube (like the lights at school).

SLOW DOWN THE MOTOR

You can slow down the motor by adding things to the circuit that will use electricity.

The light bulb, for example, will use some of the electricity.

Hook up the battery to the light, to the motor, to the push button, and back to the battery like this:

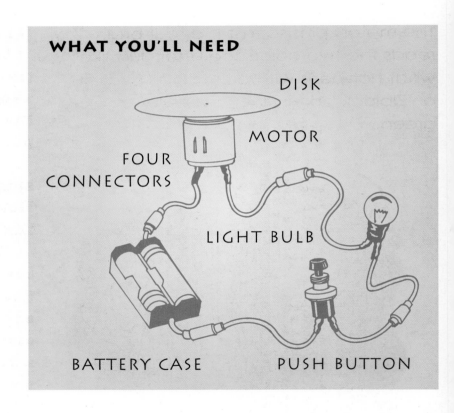

WHAT YOU'LL NEED

DISK

MOTOR

FOUR CONNECTORS

LIGHT BULB

BATTERY CASE

PUSH BUTTON

What's Going On?

Each item is strongest when it works alone because it can hog all the electricity itself. With several things in the circuit, most of the electricity can be used up by one part. (They've got to share!)

Does the light bulb seem to be dimmer or to flicker because of the motor?

Try holding the motor still. What happens to the brightness of the bulb? (It gets more of the juice.)

Remove the light from the circuit and rehook the motor. What happens?

SERIES OR PARALLEL

Until now, you have hooked all your experiments up in *series*. That means the parts are hooked up single file and the electricity flows in one big circle. Like everyone holding hands in a circle.

Another way parts can be hooked up is in *parallel*, where two paths of electricity can be happening at the same time.

Hook your motor and light bulb in a parallel circuit like this:

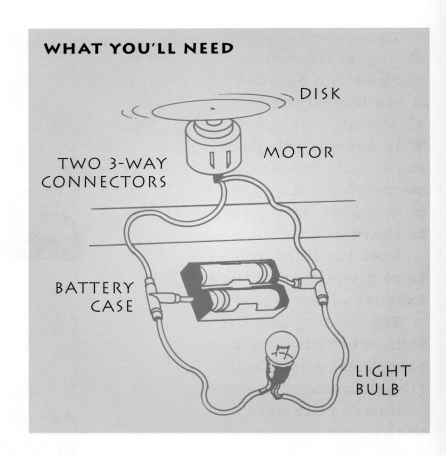

WHAT YOU'LL NEED

DISK

MOTOR

TWO 3-WAY CONNECTORS

BATTERY CASE

LIGHT BULB

What's Going On?

Parallel

Connected in parallel, each part gets all the electricity it needs. The battery makes both the motor and the bulb work strongly.

Series

Connected in series, all the parts must share one pathway of electricity.

THE ONE-WAY LIGHT

Until now all of your parts have let electricity flow through in both directions. It didn't matter how you hooked them up as long as they made a complete circuit. Now you are going to use something that's a little pickier about electricity.

Some things in your kit only work in one way. That means they allow electricity to flow in only one direction.

Take out your little red light. That is your light-emitting diode, or **LED** for short. A funny thing about the **LED** is it is a one-way light. It only lets electricity go through in one direction.

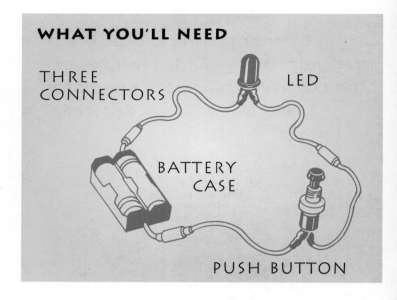

WHAT YOU'LL NEED

THREE CONNECTORS

LED

BATTERY CASE

PUSH BUTTON

Connect one of the **LED** wires to the battery case. Connect the **LED** to the switch and then to the battery case. Does it work? If it doesn't, unplug the **LED** and hook it up to the opposite wires.

Hint: the red wire of the LED should be hooked up to the red wire of the battery.

What's Going On?

LEDs give off light as the electrical current passes through. They are small, need only a small current, and last longer than light bulbs. Hold your LED up to a light. The metal inside is called a semiconductor junction (a big name for such a small part). It allows the current to pass through in only one direction.

You'll find LEDs used as on/off lights for your stereo, TV, video games, computers, VCRs, and many other places. Be a LEDetective! How many LEDs can you find around your house?

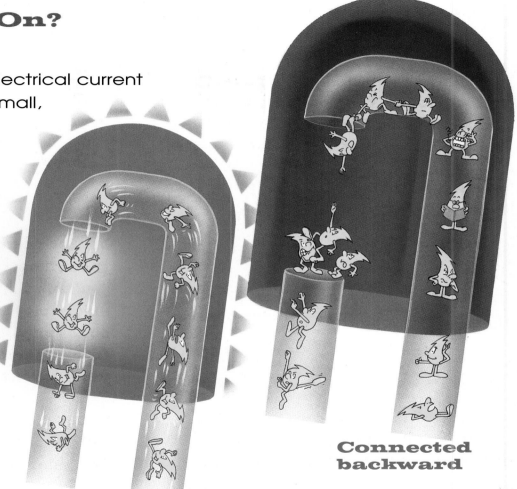

Connected correctly

Connected backward

27

YOU BUZZED?

You have another picky gadget in your toolbox. It looks like a little black can with a hole in the top. This is your buzzer. Let's make some noise!

WHAT YOU'LL NEED

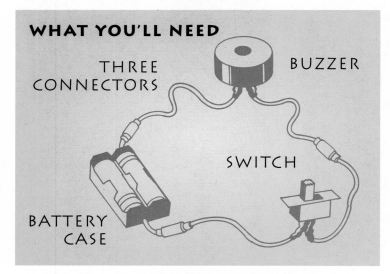

THREE CONNECTORS

BUZZER

SWITCH

BATTERY CASE

You know what to do! Use the connectors to hook the battery case, the buzzer, and the switch. Because it only works one way, the buzzer needs the red wire hooked to the red battery wire.

Since the buzzer uses a lot of electricity, and the sound is loud and obnoxious, the switch will keep you from wearing out your battery—and your parents.

Try hooking up your buzzer and LED at the same time. (Make sure you don't get one backward!)

What's Going On?

Inside the buzzer is a special disk that shakes, or vibrates, when electricity goes through it. That shaking turns electrical current into sound. (In this case, a very annoying sound.) You may have heard a sound like this when your mom or dad burned the toast and set off the smoke alarm!

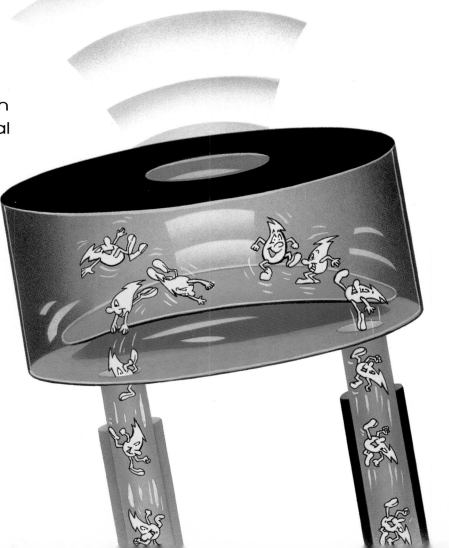

FANTASTIC CHALLENGE!

Now that you're an expert in electronics and circuitry, it's time to experiment and make something cool.

Make a fan. Punch out the paper fan blade from your cardboard box. Fold on the dotted lines so that one side folds up and the other folds down. Tape it to the motor disk. Take the motor out of the motor stand. Connect it to the battery. Can you feel the air move?

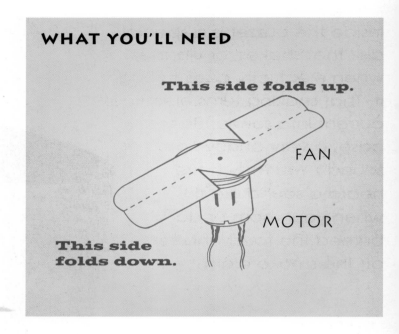

WHAT YOU'LL NEED

This side folds up.

FAN

MOTOR

This side folds down.

HELP!

If you can't make a project work, try these suggestions:

- Make sure the batteries are OK. Test them by putting the batteries in something else that uses AA batteries—a small flashlight, a toy, or a pocket video game.

- Check all your connections. Make sure all the plugs fit tightly in the connectors. Remember, electricity flows through metal.

IF A WIRE BREAKS AT A PLUG—FEAR NOT! IT CAN BE FIXED!

1. Ask an adult to strip one inch of insulation off the end of the wire.

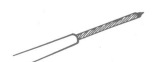

2. Twist all the stray wires together.

3. Stick the pointed wire up through the plug until it comes out of the top of the plug.

4. Fold the wires over the top of the plug.

5. It's fixed! Use it like you use the other plugs.

CONGRATULATIONS!

Congratulations, you're now an electronic wizard.

If you think this was fun, you'll LOVE *Fun with Electronics* where you get to build your very own circuit board and make 25 more amazing electronic gadgets!